# LIFE OF THE DOLPHIN

## SUE HOUGHTON

Illustrated by
### Martin Camm

## Troll Associates

*Library of Congress Cataloging-in-Publication Data*

Houghton, Sue, (date)
    Dolphin / by Sue Houghton ; illustrated by Martin Camm.
      p.    cm. — (Life story)
    Summary: Describes some different species of dolphins and their
physical characteristics, behavior, and range.
    ISBN 0-8167-2767-8 (lib. bdg.)        ISBN 0-8167-2768-6 (pbk.)
    1. Dolphins—Juvenile literature.   [1. Dolphins.]   I. Camm,
Martin, ill.   II. Title.   III. Series.
QL737.C432H68 1993
599.5'3—dc20                                        91-44819

## Published by Troll Associates

© 1994 Eagle Books

Design by James Marks
Edited by Kate Woodhouse
Picture research by Jan Croot

Printed in U.S.A.

10 9 8 7 6 5 4 3 2 1

Picture credits
Andrea/François Gohier: 5, 7, 27, 29
Horace Dobbs: cover
NHPA/Barbara Todd: 9
Planet Earth/Peter Scoones: 23
Planet Earth/Marc Webber: 19, 21
Norbert Wu: 11, 13, 15, 17, 25

# INTRODUCTION

If you've ever been lucky enough to see dolphins in the wild, you know how exciting it is to watch them leaping out of the water. Sometimes you can see them riding the waves, or twisting and rolling in the water. With their fixed smiles, they look as if they're really having fun!

Dolphins live in water like fish, but they are actually small, toothed whales. In this book you will find out how these wonderful animals live.

Risso's dolphin

Ganges river dolphin

How are dolphins different from fish? Dolphins don't have scales. They have soft, sensitive skin. They don't lay eggs but give birth to live young that feed on their mother's milk.

4

Dolphins belong to a group of animals called mammals. There are many different species of dolphins. The bottle-nosed dolphins in the photograph are among the better known. The drawings show some other kinds.

northern right-whale dolphin

rough-toothed dolphin

Dolphins breathe air. They have lungs and a blowhole —a kind of nostril — on the top of their heads. They come up to the surface to let out used air, and take in fresh air before diving underwater again. Can you see the blowholes on the common dolphins in the photograph?

Dolphins have a layer of fat under their skin, called blubber, to keep them warm. They are warm-blooded animals. This means that their body temperature stays the same however hot or cold the water. Like us, they have a body temperature of about 98°F (37°C).

Dolphins range in length from about 4 to 30 feet (1.2 to 9 meters). Porpoises, like the one below, are also toothed whales, but they are smaller than dolphins and have rounder foreheads.

Some dolphins have become river or lake dwellers, but most live in the world's oceans. Some are found in coastal waters, while others rarely venture close to land. The dusky dolphin, seen leaping in the photograph, lives in southern waters, off the south coasts of Australia, South America, and Africa.

Dolphins are streamlined like fish. Their long, narrow shape is ideal for swimming. The ease with which dolphins move helps them to catch their food and to escape from danger.

The powerful up and down movement of the dolphin's tail, or *fluke*, pushes it forward. It steers with its flippers. Most dolphins swim at about 18 miles (30 kilometers) per hour, although they can swim much faster for short periods of time. Regular leaps out of the water can increase a dolphin's speed.

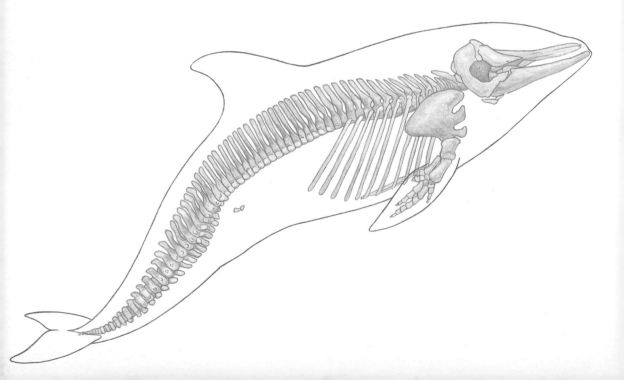

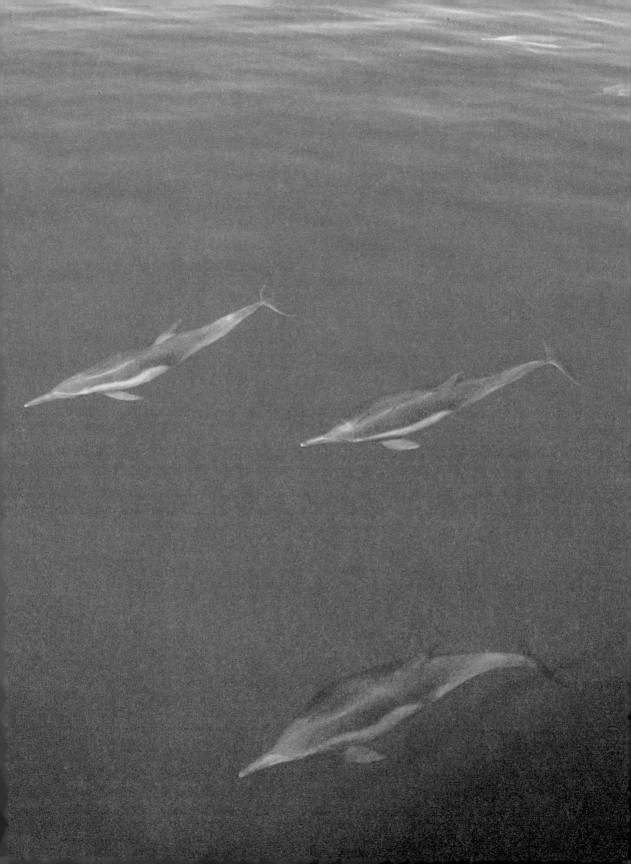

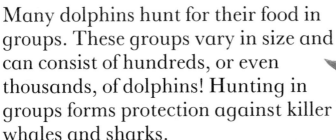

Many dolphins hunt for their food in groups. These groups vary in size and can consist of hundreds, or even thousands, of dolphins! Hunting in groups forms protection against killer whales and sharks.

12   Dusky dolphins chase schools of fish, herd them together, and trap them between themselves and the surface of the water. Bottle-nosed dolphins drive fish into shallow water to trap them.

Some dolphins also feed on squid, shrimp, octopus, and cuttlefish.

Dolphins have cone-shaped teeth.
These are ideal for catching and
holding slippery fish, but not for
chewing. Once a dolphin has caught a
fish, it usually swallows it whole,
headfirst so that the scales don't stick in
its throat.

Dolphins are camouflaged: Their
coloring and markings make it hard for
other animals to see them. This is
useful protection from enemies and
good for hunting. Usually a dolphin's
back is darker than its underside, so it
is difficult to see it from above or below.

Dolphins, like the Amazon dolphin in the photograph, have small eyes. But most dolphins can see fairly well both in and out of water. However, they find it hard to judge distance. To solve this problem, they use a special skill.

As a dolphin moves forward it sends out clicking sounds from a fatty area in its head, called the melon. When the sound hits an object, echoes bounce back. The length of time between the clicks and the echoes gives the dolphin a clear picture of the distance and size of the object. The ability to use sound in this way is called echolocation.

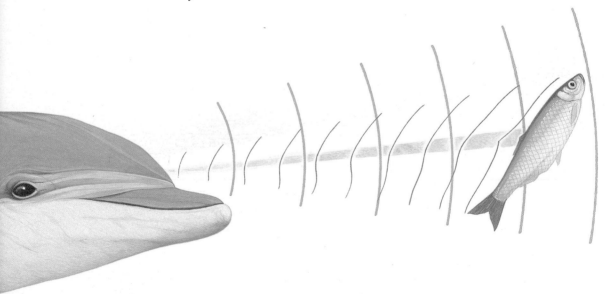

The dolphin's ability to find fish is useful to other animals. Sea birds and tuna often follow dolphins to pick up fish that are being trapped. Fishermen know this and use the dolphins to find tuna, because the dolphins are easy to spot when they surface for air. Sadly, the nets also catch the dolphins. Some improvements to net design have been made to prevent the needless killing of so many dolphins, but there is still much to be done.

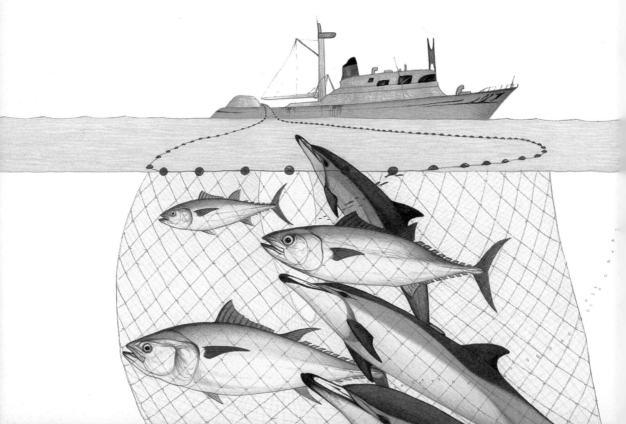

Dolphins play throughout their lives,
especially when they are looking for a
mate. The male does most of the
chasing, showing off to the females
with jumps and spins. He will also
gently stroke and rub the female with
his head.

Dolphins mate and produce young when they are between five and sixteen years old. The length of pregnancy varies between different species, but some last up to 16 months. The mother usually gives birth to only one calf. As the drawing shows, the calf is born tailfirst. As soon as it is born, the mother and other females, or "aunts," push the calf to the surface so that it takes its first breath very quickly.

For the first few weeks the calf needs to breathe every 30 seconds and feed every 30 minutes. The calf gets rich milk from its mother.

A calf sometimes stays with its mother for as long as six years. It is also looked after by the "aunts" and protected by the rest of the group. If an enemy approaches, the mother and young are safe in the middle of the group.

By the time it is two years old, the calf has learned a great deal. It usually learns through play, where touching is important. The bottle-nosed dolphin here is investigating a stone, using the sensitive skin of its lower jaw. The calf communicates with its mother by touching, whistles, and squeaks.

Some people think dolphins are intelligent, because they have large brains compared with other mammals. Their great ability to learn and to mimic never fails to interest people.

Killer whales, like this one, are the largest members of the dolphin family. Sometimes they are kept in captivity to perform tricks. Dolphins are also used to perform tasks impossible for human divers. Many people feel this is wrong, but others argue that it is a way of learning more about dolphins. What do you think?

There are many stories based on people's friendships with dolphins. At one time, it was thought to be bad luck to kill dolphins because they were humans in another form.

Dolphins are social animals, like us, and help each other when injured. There are even reports of them rescuing humans from drowning! But there is still a lot to be discovered.

Many human activities affect dolphins. We must ensure that their grace and beauty remain with us in the years to come.

# Fact file

The killer whale is the fastest water mammal, reaching speeds of up to 35 miles per hour (55 km/h). Most of the other dolphins swim at about 18 mph (30 km/h), which is still three times faster than the fastest human swimmer.

The killer whale is also the highest jumper. It can reach 18 feet (5.5 meters). The bottle-nosed dolphin is not far behind, with a record of 15 feet (4.6 meters).

One of the great mysteries of whale and dolphin behavior is mass strandings, when hundreds of them swim onto beaches for no apparent reason.

Once they are on the beach, or in very shallow water, they can't get back out to sea, and they die. The animals are usually found to be healthy. One theory about this is that the dolphins somehow become confused by the Earth's magnetic field. Another is that there may be a fault in the echolocation sense of these animals.

Dolphins don't sleep for long periods of time, but rest just under the surface of the water so that they can breathe air every two to three minutes. When awake, a dolphin can hold its breath for up to ten minutes.

Unlike us, dolphins can't breathe through their mouths. This means that when they feed, water can't enter their lungs and drown them.

31

# Index